D1404390

Animal Habitats

The Bat in the Cave

Text by Helen Riley

Photographs by
Oxford Scientific Films

Gareth Stevens Publishing
Milwaukee

Contents

Note: The use of a capital letter for a bat's name means that it is a specific *type* (or species) of bat (for example, Noctule Bat). The use of a lowercase, or small, letter means that it is a member of a larger *group* of bats.

Bats flying out of the Tamana Cave in Trinidad in the West Indies.

A cluster of Long-fingered Bats roosting in a cave.

Bats and their homes

Bats are the only mammals that can fly. In textbooks you will often find them referred to as *Chiroptera*. This is a Greek word that means "hand-wing." It describes bats well because their wings are pieces of thin, elastic skin stretched between their very long finger bones.

Bats are active only at night. They spend the daylight hours tucked away in an enclosed, dark space. They like to use caves and crevices in rocks, but in some parts of the world there are few natural caves. So bats will also live in burrows dug by other animals, in hollows in trees, and in a variety of cave-like places such as abandoned mine shafts or the roof spaces of buildings. Holy places seem to be popular; churches, ancient temples, and even the burial chambers of the Egyptian pyramids are all regularly used by bats.

A *roost* may contain anything from one bat to many thousands of bats. Inside the roost, bats do very little except rest for most of the day. They either tuck themselves out of sight into crevices in the wall or hang — upside down — from the walls or ceiling. As dusk falls, they wake up and fly out of the roost to feed, usually returning just before dawn. They therefore spend practically all their lives in darkness, dividing their time between the roost and the open night air.

Bats are curious and fascinating animals, well adapted to their strange *nocturnal* way of life.

Bats around the world

There are about 950 *species* of bats. They are divided into two main groups — *Megachiroptera* (which means "big hand-wing") and *Microchiroptera* ("small hand-wing").

Megachiroptera, or megabats, have large eyes, long noses, and foxy ears. They usually feed on fruit, which is why they are often called fruit bats or flying foxes. They live in the *tropical* regions of Africa, Asia, Australia, and Indonesia, and they usually roost in hollows in trees or in the open, where they hang upside down from tree branches. On the whole, they are larger than Microchiroptera, and this group includes the biggest bat of all, the Samoan Flying Fox. This bat has a wingspan of up to 5 ft (1.5 m) and weighs about 3 lbs (1.5 kg) — about the size of a chicken with extremely long wings!

Most bats (about 780 species) belong to the Microchiroptera, or microbats, which are more widely distributed than megabats. Microbats live just about everywhere on the land surface of the world, except for the polar regions, the tops of the highest mountains, and the remotest islands. Most are small to medium-sized — which, for a bat, means a body of about the size and shape of a mouse or a rat, and a wingspan of less than 18 inches (50 cm). Microchiroptera tend to have flat faces with tiny eyes and fairly large ears, and most species feed on insects and other small animals.

Like all megabats, these Egyptian Fruit Bats have large eyes that are adapted for seeing in very dim light.

The Noctule is a species of microbat that lives in Europe.

In many species of mammals males and females look quite different. Males may be bigger than females and perhaps have distinct features, like the antlers of a stag or the mane of a lion. But in most species of bats, males and females are about the same size, shape, and color. Color does not vary very much in bats either — their coats are usually brown or gray. Most bats spend their lives in the dark and are colorblind, so brightly colored coats and differences in body shape between males and females would not be of much use. Other bats would not be able to see them. The senses of hearing and smell are more useful than sight to most bats.

Some species of megabats roost out in the open, hanging from the branches of trees. These Gray-headed Flying Foxes live in Australia.

This Naked-backed Bat is echolocating before flying. Its ears are pricked forward to listen for echoes.

Finding a way in the dark

Microbats have tiny eyes that are not much use in the dark. Instead, they use a special system, called *echolocation*, to find their way around and search for food. While flying, microbats continually produce clicking noises from their throats. These noises are *ultrasonic*, which means they are of too high a pitch for the human ear to hear, but perfectly audible to bats with their extremely sensitive ears. When the sounds hit an obstacle in the bats' flight path they are reflected back as echoes. By listening carefully to these echoes, bats can tell the size, shape, and texture of objects they are flying toward, and whether those objects are moving or staying still. They can therefore tell the difference between something they should dodge, like the branch of a tree, and something good to eat, like a moth, that should be chased and caught.

Some microbats have really odd-shaped faces that are specially adapted for echolocation. Their ears are often large, and inside the main earlobe is a small, upright flap of skin called a tragus, which seems to help the bat tell which direction an echo is coming from. Some bats, like horseshoe and Leaf-chinned Bats, also have a strangely shaped flap of skin surrounding their nose or mouth. These rather bizarre adornments focus and direct the sounds that the bats make.

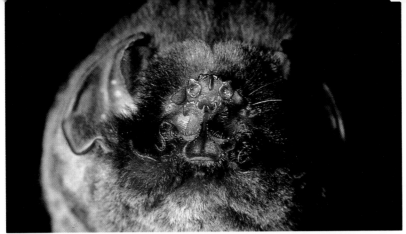

Scientists believe that the curiously shaped flaps of skin on the faces of Leaf-chinned Bats help them produce their echolocation sounds.

Although megabats are also nocturnal, most of them cannot echolocate. Even at night there is some light from the moon and stars, and the large eyes of fruit bats and flying foxes are designed to make the most of very dim light. They use a combination of sight and a well-developed sense of smell to seek out their food.

The Rousette Fruit Bats are the only megabats that can echolocate, and they use a much simpler system than microbats. They produce sounds with their tongues, and these clicks are not ultrasonic (humans can hear them). Rousette Fruit Bats are also the only megabats that regularly live in caves where no light penetrates. They only echolocate inside their roost. Once outside, they "switch off" their navigation noises and use their eyes instead.

Like birds, different species of bats produce different sounds, and with a little practice it is possible to distinguish between some (unfortunately not all) species of microbat with the help of a bat detector. This is a special kind of transistor radio that converts ultrasonic sounds into noises that humans can hear. Scientists studying bats find this device very useful because small flying bats are extremely difficult to identify by sight.

Brown Long-eared Bats have big ears so they can pick up even the faintest of echoes.

The body of a bat

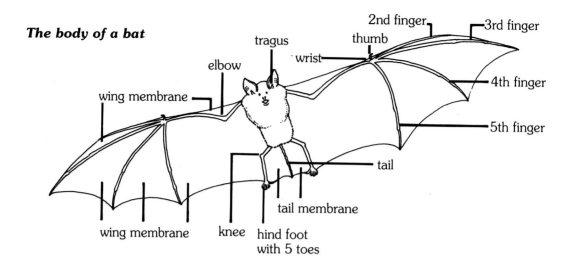

2nd finger
thumb
3rd finger
tragus
wrist
elbow
wing membrane
4th finger
5th finger
tail
tail membrane
wing membrane   knee   hind foot
with 5 toes

Moving about

Bats have very long forelimbs compared to the rest of their body. The bones of their fingers are especially long and act as supports for their wings, in the same way that the spokes support an umbrella. The wing is a thin piece of skin stretching from the sides of the body and the short back legs, along the forearm, and over the fingers. It also stretches over the bottom of the thumb. The end of the thumb sticks out of the front edge of the wing membrane and has a claw at its tip. A flap of the wing membrane may also stretch between the back legs, and in microbats the tail usually runs down the middle of this membrane. Many megabats do not have tails and their wing membranes do not extend between their back legs.

Bats fly in much the same way as birds. They first raise and fully extend their wings and then sweep them downward and forward. This downstroke creates the "lift" that keeps the bat in the air. The wings are then brought upwards and backwards in a recovery stroke, ready for the next downstroke.

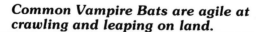

Common Vampire Bats are agile at crawling and leaping on land.

The five claws on bats' back feet allow them to grip tightly to the roof of their roost.

Bats fly more slowly and are more agile than birds. They need to be! Birds generally fly during the daytime and have excellent eyesight. They can spot obstacles long before they reach them. Bats fly in darkness, and they cannot detect objects in their path until they are close to them. They need to be able to change direction very quickly.

Bats vary in their flying ability and the shape of their wings depending on the life they lead. Slow, agile fliers like Greater Horseshoe Bats catch insects in the air and have short, broad wings. Mexican Free-tailed Bats and other fast-flying bats that need to cover long distances have long, narrow wings.

Bats are much less graceful on the ground than in the air, although they can crawl around quite rapidly. They fold their wing membranes out of the way to stop them from being damaged, and they bear most of their weight on their forelegs. Their hind legs are shorter and spindlier and usually stick out sideways or backwards, rather than being held underneath their bodies. Each hind leg has five toes with claws that are used for clinging to surfaces like the rocky walls of a cave or the wooden beams inside the roof of a house.

When coming to rest, bats often land head upward, clinging on with their thumbs. They turn to hang from their back feet with their heads downward. This sounds like a very awkward position to rest in. But bats' back legs are designed so the weight of the body pulls on the feet and causes the toes to curl up and grip tightly. So even when it falls asleep, a bat need not worry about falling from its roost!

This Greater Horseshoe Bat is just about to catch a moth.

Feeding on animals

Most bats are *insectivorous* — they eat insects and other small invertebrate animals like spiders or scorpions. These bats have teeth with sharp, ridged surfaces, which are useful for biting and cutting up *prey*.

If you watch insectivorous bats flying you will see them wheeling, dodging, and swooping through the air, changing direction rapidly almost as though they are tied to a piece of string being jerked by someone at the other end of it. What they are doing is chasing after insects like moths, beetles, and flies, using echolocation to home in on their prey. Their flying ability is tested to the utmost as the hunted insects try to avoid them.

Usually, bats catch insects in their mouths, sometimes using their wings to sweep prey into their waiting jaws. Some bats also use the flap of wing membrane between their hind legs to help catch prey. This membrane can be folded forward over the belly to form a pouch to hold a struggling insect. The bat dips its head into the pouch repeatedly to snatch bites, and manages to do this without flying into anything!

Some bats pick unsuspecting insects from leaves, or from the ground. Brown Long-eared Bats fly slowly among the branches of trees, snatching prey from the surfaces of leaves. Pallid Bats hunt low over the ground, swooping onto scorpions, grasshoppers, and beetles. Daubenton's Bats skim over water, picking off beetles and emerging insects like caddis flies.

The bigger the bat, the bigger the prey it can tackle. Some of the larger microbats feed on larger animals than insects. Fisherman Bats, which live in the American tropics, use echolocation to detect the ripples made by fish at the surface of water. They then swoop low over the surface and hook out the fish with the sharp claws of their hind feet. The Australian False Vampire Bat, the largest of the microbats, hunts mice, frogs, birds, and lizards, and it may even kill and eat other bats.

The true vampire bats of South America are well known for their gruesome habit of feeding on blood. The Common Vampire Bat usually attacks farm animals such as cows, pigs, or donkeys. It makes a small wound on its sleeping victim with its sharp teeth and laps blood with its tongue. A special substance in its saliva stops the blood from clotting. The vampire may take in about half its own weight in a single feed, but this is a small loss for the animal it feeds from. More threatening are diseases like rabies which vampire bats may carry and pass on to any animal they bite. For this reason vampires are one of the few bat species that can be truly considered as pests.

A Pipistrelle Bat showing off its set of sharp teeth. It uses them to slice through the tough outer skins of insects.

This Fisherman Bat has just made a successful catch. It has large back feet with sharp, curved claws for hooking fish out of the water.

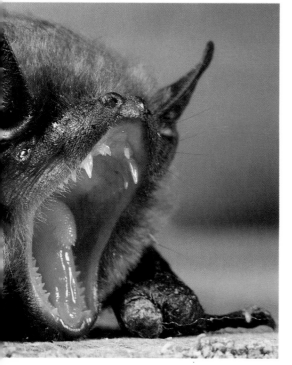

This Little Fruit-eating Bat looks as though it may have bitten off more than it can chew!

Feeding on plants

Bats that feed on plants eat fruits or flowers. This includes nearly all fruit bats and flying foxes (megabats), and some species of spear-nosed bats (microbats) that live in Central and South America. These bats live only in tropical areas of the world, because only there is the climate warm enough for there to be fruits and flowers present year-round.

Frugivorous (fruit-eating) bats like soft, ripe fruits which they don't need to chew. Instead, they crush them to a pulp with their flat-topped teeth and swallow the sugary juices, later spitting out the chewed-up flesh.

A useful spin-off for a plant is that a bat eating its fruits may help to spread its seeds. The bat either carries the fruit away from the parent tree and drops the seeds before eating it, or it swallows small seeds along with the fruit juices and later passes them out, unharmed, in its droppings. The Straw-colored Flying Fox, a common species from West Africa, helps to disperse the seeds of many plants of the tropical forest and grassland. This feeding arrangement benefits both parties. The bat gets fed, and the plants get their seeds carried to new areas.

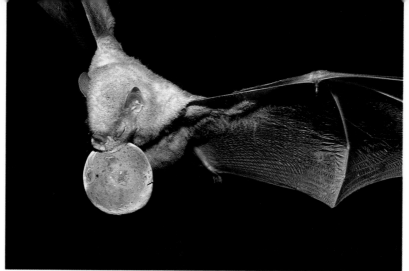

By carrying a fig away, this Spear-nosed Bat is helping to disperse the seeds of the fig tree.

Bats that feed from flowers are actually searching for nectar and *pollen*. They have long tongues with bristly ends that they use to reach right down into the bottoms of flowers. This is where the nectar is found. Mexican Long-nosed Bats spend their summers in the deserts of Arizona feeding on giant Saguaro Cacti. They travel in flocks from plant to plant, but because they cannot hover like hummingbirds do, they must swoop repeatedly down over flowers, each time snatching a mouthful of nectar or pollen.

Plants may also benefit from the visits of nectar-seeking bats because pollen that sticks to the bats' fur may be carried from one flower to another. When a flower receives pollen from a different flower of the same species, its seeds can become fertilized. Many tropical plants have become specially adapted to be *pollinated* by bats. They have large, pungent-smelling flowers that only open up at night when bats are feeding.

The long tongue of this Mexican Long-nosed Bat is used to reach down to the bottoms of flowers and lap up nectar. The yellow dust on its fur is pollen.

This hibernating Daubenton's Bat is covered with droplets of condensed water.

Surviving the winter

Like all mammals, bats are warm-blooded. They can keep their body temperature at the same level despite changes in the surrounding temperature. In cold weather, however, some species of bats are able to cool their bodies down to almost the same temperature as their surroundings. They can stay in this condition for days or weeks at a stretch. When this happens, a bat is said to be in *hibernation*.

These Indiana Bats have clustered together to hibernate.

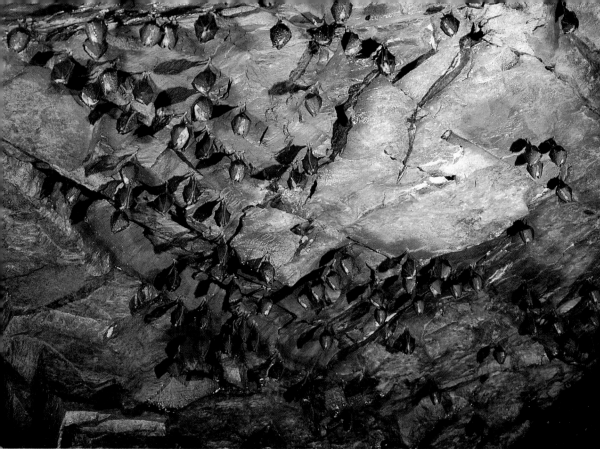

A group of Lesser Horseshoe Bats hibernating in an unused mine shaft.

Only bats living in *temperate* areas of the world need to hibernate. During the cold winter months their food supply — flying insects — is so scarce that if they remained active they would probably starve. Instead they build up stores of fat in their bodies during the late summer and autumn. By hibernating, they can make a little fat go a long way. The lower the temperature at which they hibernate, the longer their fat reserves will last.

A hibernating bat looks dead. It feels cold and clammy, and its fur is often covered with droplets of condensed water. But inside, its body is still working very slowly. Its heart rate, for example, has dropped from about 400 beats per minute when awake, to about 25 beats per minute. By slowing down the internal working of its body, the bat uses up the energy in its stored fat reserves at a very slow rate.

Obviously, the place a bat chooses to hibernate must be cool. It should also be humid, so the bat doesn't lose water rapidly and have to wake up frequently to drink. Hibernating bats also need places where other animals can't find them. A hibernating bat takes at least half an hour to wake up fully, by which time it could have been eaten if it was found by a *predator*.

You can see how this Lesser Horseshoe Bat wraps its wings right around its body.

Caves provide excellent hibernating places for bats because the temperature inside stays cool and fairly constant throughout the winter. Some species hang from the roof or walls, either singly — like Greater Horseshoe Bats — or in clusters — like Gray Bats and Long-fingered Bats. Others, such as Daubenton's Bats, tuck themselves into crevices in the walls. Although caves are usually humid places, most hibernating bats fold their wings out of the way because water is quickly lost from such large areas of naked skin. Horseshoe bats, however, prefer to wrap their wings right around their bodies and hang from the ceiling like folded-up umbrellas, but they only hibernate in very humid caves.

Some bats, like Brown Long-eared Bats and Barbastelles, only hibernate in caves when the weather gets really cold. For the rest of the winter they hibernate in trees, where they move into hollows in the trunk or crevices in the bark. Trees are generally colder and drier places to hibernate in than caves, and the temperature also tends to fluctuate a bit more, but the cooler a bat gets the slower it uses up its fat reserves. Tree hibernators seem to be able to put up with temperatures down to about 22°F (-5.6°C), below the freezing point of water. If it gets colder, they usually move into caves.

In Europe and North America, bats enter hibernation in September or October and emerge in April or May. So hibernation lasts six or seven months. Bats do not hibernate continuously, but wake up at intervals. They may move and continue hibernating in a different place or, if the temperature has warmed a little, they may fly out in search of food. On a warm winter day there may be enough insects around to provide a hungry bat with a square meal. Winter feeding sessions may be vital for survival if a bat is running low on stored fat.

Although they do wake up of their own accord, hibernating bats, if found, should not be disturbed. Just a touch may be enough to rouse them (even though they do not seem to react immediately), and in waking up they use up much of their stored fat. If conditions are not good enough for them to feed and replace the lost energy, they may die before the winter is through.

Most bats, like this Natterer's Bat, fold their wings out of the way when they hibernate.

The breeding season

Bats that live in temperate countries must time their breeding seasons correctly. Only during the short summer months is there enough food around (in the form of flying insects) for females to raise their young successfully. For example, in northern Europe bats come out of hibernation in April. They have only five months until they must hibernate once again, and during this time the young must be born, suckled, *weaned,* and taught to fly and feed for themselves. There is only just enough time for each female to have one litter.

A year in the life of the Greater Horseshoe Bat, which lives in temperate areas of Europe and Asia.

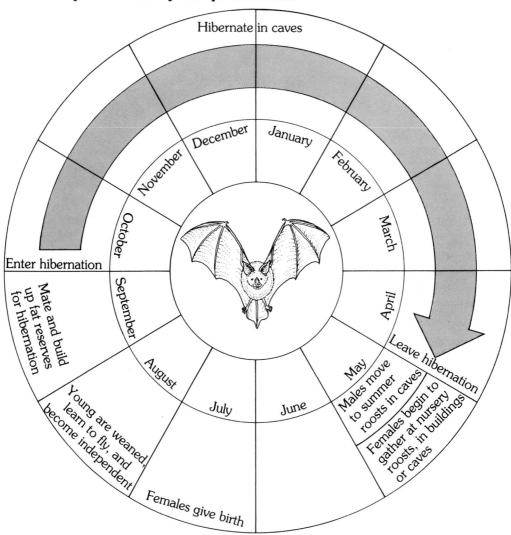

The Greater Horseshoe Bat.

It is important that the *embryo* bats begin developing in the female's body as soon as possible after she emerges from hibernation. To achieve this, mating actually takes place in the autumn and winter. Once a female bat has received sperm from a male one of two things may happen. The sperm may be stored in her *uterus* while she hibernates, ready to fertilize the ripe egg cells she produces the following spring. Or, the eggs may be fertilized soon after mating but remain undeveloped in the uterus over the winter. In either case, the females don't have to waste time searching for a mate in the spring because they are already pregnant.

In some tropical countries the climate and food supply for bats are much the same all year round. Young bats may be born in any month of the year, although the females of one species usually all give birth together at about the same time each year. In other tropical regions, however, the rainfall varies throughout the year. In some months it will rain almost every day, while in other months it may not rain at all. This variation in rainfall means that the food supply for bats (whether they eat insects, fruits, or flowers) is more abundant at certain times of year. Bats living in these areas arrange their breeding seasons so they give birth to their young at the time that their food supply is most plentiful.

Once they have mated, the male of this pair of Leaf-chinned Bats will go looking for other females to mate with. He does not help bring up the baby bats he has fathered.

Mating and giving birth

Male and female bats usually come together only briefly to mate. There is very little in the way of courtship, and the two do not stay together for long. The female later brings up her offspring without any help from the father. This situation is taken to extremes in Mexican Free-tailed Bats. Males and females overwinter in Mexico, where they mate. The females then fly north a thousand miles (1,600 km) or so into Texas where they give birth to their young, while many of the males stay behind to spend the summer in Mexico.

Pregnant female bats of the same species usually gather into nursery colonies to give birth and to raise their young. These groups of females vary from fewer than ten to several million bats! Nursery colonies often form in caves, but nowadays the roof spaces of houses are becoming popular places, perhaps because they are warmer than caves in summer. The warmer it is, the faster the baby bats grow.

A nursery colony of female Long-eared Bats in the loft of a country house.

Because a pregnant female bat has to be able to fly, she cannot have many young inside her at once, or she would become too heavy to take off! Other small to medium-sized mammals (mice or rabbits, for example) generally produce litters of between four and eight young, but female bats usually have only one or sometimes two babies at a time. Only a few species of North American bats, like the Red Bat, are known to regularly produce three or four young at once.

Baby bats are born in the nursery roost. The female may give birth as she hangs upside down, but some bats, including the Noctule Bat, turn to hang head up before giving birth. The mother then catches the youngster in her tail membrane after it has emerged.

A small nursery colony of female Daubenton's Bats.

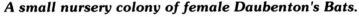

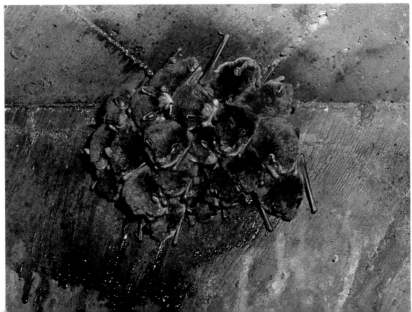

Growing up

Baby bats enter the world naked and blind, but they are not entirely helpless. Like all baby mammals, they are fed for a while on milk produced by their mother, and they are born with a full set of milk teeth so they can suckle right away. They also have well-developed back feet so they can cling to their mother and to the roof of the nursery roost. If they fall to the floor while their mother is out feeding they may die before she returns.

Female bats are sometimes seen carrying their young, but this probably only happens when the baby bats are very young, or if the females are moving to a new nursery roost. Baby bats soon grow to be too heavy to be carried for any length of time, so they are left behind while their mothers go out to feed. All the youngsters from one nursery roost huddle together for warmth and protection. They are very noisy, and it is probably partially by their calls that the returning mothers recognize their own babies.

These seven-day-old Gould's Long-eared Bats are firmly attached to their mother.

This baby Brown Long-eared Bat sheltering beneath its mother is nearly fully grown.

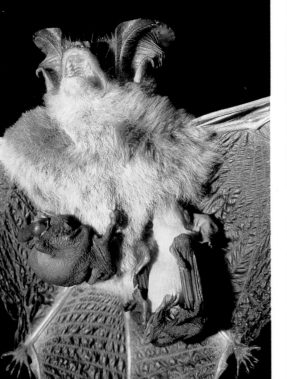

*You can imagine how hard it would be
for this female to fly and carry her babies.
They are only a week old but are already
nearly as big as their mother.*

The babies of small species of bat like Pipistrelles and Noctules develop very quickly. Hair begins to grow on their backs in their first week of life, and by the end of their second week they are fully covered with fur (apart from their wings, of course) and their eyes have opened. They soon become active, grooming themselves, crawling around and stretching their wings. Three weeks to a month after they have been born, the young bats make their first flights, and they soon start to fly out at night to feed with their mothers. By this time they have been weaned and their milk teeth have fallen out and have been replaced by a set of permanent, adult teeth. Six weeks to two months after birth, the young bats are fully grown.

The young of larger bats take longer to develop. It may be three months before the babies of some of the bigger species of flying foxes take to the air. But the slowest developer among bats is actually one of the smaller species. Baby vampire bats stay with their mothers for nine months or even more. They are suckled for three months, and after that they are gradually weaned onto a diet of blood.

The bond between a mother bat and her young is usually strong while the baby is still suckling. This is not so, however, in the large nursery colonies of species like the Mexican Free-tailed Bat. Here, there may be thousands of mothers and babies living together, so many that it would take a very long time for a mother returning from feeding to find her own baby. Instead, females just adopt the first couple of baby bats they come across. In this way, each youngster gets fed — even if not by its own mother!

An Oilbird perched on its nest deep inside a cave.

Bats, birds, and other cave dwellers

On the whole, caves are rather barren places. No light penetrates beyond a short distance inside the entrance, which means that no green plants can grow. So most caves, particularly in temperate regions, contain very few living creatures simply because there is nothing to eat inside the cave. Bats use caves as safe places in which to spend the daytime, to hibernate through the winter, and to rear their young. They must always move out of caves to find food.

Few animals rely on caves to live as heavily as bats do. There are a few species of birds that have adopted a "batty" way of life. An example is the Oilbird, which lives in tropical South America. During the daytime it roosts deep within caves, and it emerges at night to search for its food of oily fruits and nuts. Oilbirds have developed the ability to echolocate, using a system similar to that of Rousette Fruit Bats. They produce sharp, rattling calls that are not ultrasonic, and they only echolocate within the pitch darkness of their cave homes. Once outside, they use sight and smell to find their food.

These beetle larvae live in a pile of bat guano on the floor of a South American cave.

In some large caves in tropical countries bats form the basis for complicated food chains. Or rather, their *guano* does. A good example is Tamana Cave in Trinidad in the West Indies. Tamana Cave is home to thousands of bats belonging to eleven species — so many bats that it takes three hours for them all to pass through the cave entrance when they fly out to feed each night! The droppings of these bats accumulate on the cave floor in huge piles and form a food source for a multitude of worms, beetles, bugs, springtails, centipedes, millipedes, woodlice, ticks, spiders, and giant cockroaches over 2 inches (5 cm) long! Many of these invertebrates, like the springtails, feed on the tiny organisms (fungi and bacteria) that break down the guano. Others, like the spiders, feed on the smaller insects.

These creatures are eaten, in turn, by larger animals, including the Freshwater Land Crab, which lives in the stream flowing through the cave, and a small cave-dwelling frog. The tadpoles of this frog also inhabit the stream and are eaten by the resident Coral Snakes.

These are just a few of the bats that live in Tamana Cave.

Threats to bats

There are few animals that specialize in feeding on bats. Bats are not easily caught because most of them spend the daytime hidden away in a secure roost and only fly by night. However, owls and other nocturnal predators will take them if they get the chance. Also, animals like weasels and snakes may climb into roosts and kill bats.

The worst enemies of bats are people. All over the world, bats are declining in numbers, and unfortunately it is mainly humans that are responsible for this.

People hunt bats for a number of reasons. Some are considered to be pests. These are mainly fruit bats which come into conflict with people because they like to eat the same things. Egyptian Fruit Bats have been destroyed in large numbers because orchards of ripening fruit proved too much of a temptation for them. The killing, which was done by flooding the cave roosts of the bats with poisonous gases, did not really affect the numbers of Egyptian Fruit Bats very much. But other, rarer species of bat that shared the same roosts have been seriously reduced in numbers.

Barn owls and other birds of prey sometimes kill bats.

Pictures of wicked-looking bats, like this one, are often found in old books. Do you think it looks like the real bats that are pictured in this book?

Many bats have suffered because of the harm people have done to the environment. Tropical forests are being cut down at an alarming rate to provide land for farming and for building towns and cities. In temperate countries, changes in farming methods are taking place, including the removal of hedgerows and woodland. The loss of these natural *habitats* reduces the food supply for bats living in the area and also destroys the homes of bats that spend all or part of their lives roosting in trees.

Even the cave roosts of bats are not safe. People often enter caves to explore them, which disturbs any bats roosting or hibernating there. Worse still, caves may be used as places to dump rubbish, or the entrance tunnels may be sealed off if the cave is thought to be unsafe.

The use of pesticides is another threat to bats. If a bat eats many insects containing small amounts of a pesticide the poisonous chemicals will gradually build up inside its body. It may not die immediately, but it will become more susceptible to stress or disease and perhaps be unable to breed successfully. Mexican Free-tailed Bats, which used to be common in Central America, have been drastically reduced in numbers because of the use of pesticides.

A 19th-century artist has used the figure of a flying bat to create an eerie and mysterious atmosphere in this engraving.

Sadly, bats are also persecuted because many people fear and misunderstand them. In the past, bats have been regarded as rather sinister creatures and associated with witchcraft, the devil, and evil fictional characters like Dracula. In many areas of the world bats have taken to living in buildings, sometimes because their natural roosting places have been destroyed, but also because buildings provide good, warm places to breed. Although they do no harm, they are often driven away or killed just because the owners of the building don't like their being there. Sometimes the house owners may kill their bats without meaning to, by having the timbers of their roof treated with wood preservatives that are poisonous to bats.

A golden bat with wings outstretched decorates a French chalice from the early 19th century.

In many parts of the world, bat boxes are being put up to provide extra homes for bats that spend all or part of their lives roosting in trees.

Things are not all bad for bats. In many countries of the world, they are now protected by law, and groups of people who are interested in bats have gotten together to form societies to protect bats and their roosts. For example, in Europe, the entrances to many cave roosts of bats have been closed off with metal gratings. This allows the bats to enter but keeps people out.

Bats really don't deserve the bad reputation they seem to have acquired. They are clean, attractive animals, and they cause little or no harm to human beings. They may even do some good, because they eat many of the insect pests in our homes, gardens, and fields.

Life in the cave

Bats feed on insects they catch *outside* the cave. Their guano supports the food chain *inside* the cave.

The Tamana Cave Food Chain

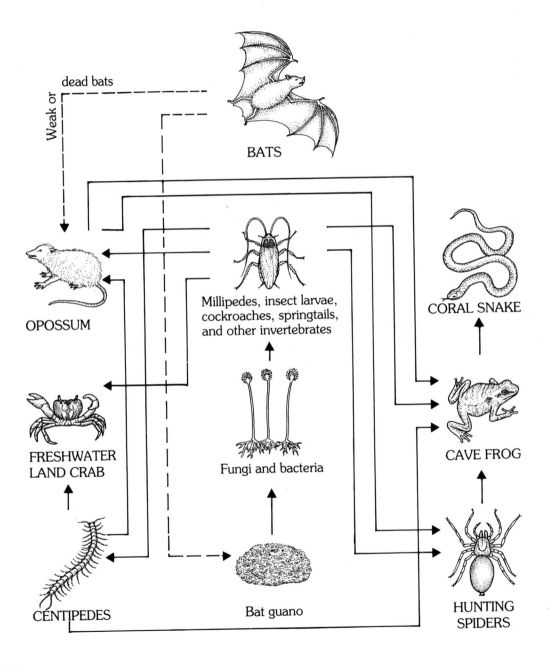

Weak or dead bats

BATS

OPOSSUM

Millipedes, insect larvae, cockroaches, springtails, and other invertebrates

CORAL SNAKE

FRESHWATER LAND CRAB

Fungi and bacteria

CAVE FROG

CENTIPEDES

Bat guano

HUNTING SPIDERS

As dusk falls, thousands of Wrinkle-lipped Bats fly out from their cave roost to feed.

As we have seen, most bat species use caves at some time in their lives. They may use the same cave the whole year round, or use different caves for hibernating and rearing their young, or perhaps move out of caves into buildings or trees to rear their young.

Nowadays, bats are protected by law in many countries of the world. But simply preventing people from killing bats is not enough. The places in which they live and their food supplies must also be protected, and to do this properly we need to find out more about bats. Perhaps most important of all, people must learn to live alongside these winged, furry, and fascinating animals.

Glossary and Index

These new words about bats appear in the text on the pages shown after each definition. Each new word first appears in the text in *italics*, just as it appears here.

Reading level analysis: SPACHE 3.6, FRY 5.5, FLESCH 81 (easy), RAYGOR 5, FOG 8

Library of Congress Cataloging-in-Publication Data

Riley, Helen.

    The bat in the cave / words by Helen Riley ; photographs by Oxford Scientific Films.

        p.   cm. — (Animal habitats)

    Summary: Text and photographs depict bats feeding, breeding, and defending themselves in their natural habitats.

    ISBN 0-8368-0112-1

    1. Bats—Juvenile literature. [1. Bats.] I. Oxford Scientific Films. II. Title. III. Series.

QL737.C5R49   1989

599.4—dc20   89-4469

North American edition first published in 1989 by Gareth Stevens, Inc., 7317 West Green Tree Road, Milwaukee, WI 53223, USA

Text copyright © 1989 by Oxford Scientific Films. All rights reserved. No part of this book may be reproduced in any form or by any means without permission in writing from Gareth Stevens, Inc.

Conceived, designed, and produced by Belitha Press Ltd., London.

Consultant Editor: Jennifer Coldrey. Art Director: Treld Bicknell. Design: Naomi Games. US Editor: Mark J. Sachner. Line Drawings: Lorna Turpin.

The authors and publishers wish to thank the following for permission to reproduce copyright material: **Oxford Scientific Films Ltd.** for front cover, pp. 8 and 10 (Stephen Dalton); pp. 2, 13 below, and 25 (J. A. L. Cooke); p. 3 (C. and D. Broomhall); p. 4 (Anthony Bannister); title page, pp. 5 above, 22 right, 29, and 31 (Alastair Shay); back cover, pp. 5 below and 22 left (Kathie Atkinson); pp. 6 and 12 (Richard Laval); p. 7 above (Robert W. Mitchell); pp. 7 below and 21 below (Press-tige Pictures); pp. 9, 11 left, 14 above, 15, 16, 17, 19, 21 above (Richard Packwood); p. 11 right (Partridge Films Ltd.); p. 13 above (David Thompson); p. 14 below (Lynn M. Stone); p. 20 (Raymond A. Mendez); p. 23 (E. R. Degginger); p. 24 above (M. P. L. Fogden); p. 24 below (G. I. Bernard); p. 26 (Mark Hamblin). Mary Evans Picture Library for p. 28 above, and C. F. L. Giraudon, Paris, for p. 28 below. Page 27 courtesy of Ben Gaskell.

Printed in the United States of America

1 2 3 4 5 6 7 8 9 95 94 93 92 91 90 89

For a free color catalog describing Gareth Stevens' list of high-quality children's books call 1 (800) 433-0942